Taking Hill 407: Mont Saint Jean

The Service of Dr. Ernest V. Orsi and Company L, 317th Infantry Regiment

Alexander Prezioso

ISBN: 978-1-300-63423-2 (Paperback)
ISBN: 979-8-317-61792-9 (Hardcover)

Dedication

This book is dedicated to both of my grandfathers, Dr. Ernest V. Orsi and Eugene Prezioso, and to the brave men of Company L, 317th Infantry Regiment, who fought with unwavering courage and resilience during the capture of Mont Saint Jean during World War II. Their sacrifices, their unwavering commitment to duty in the face of overwhelming odds, and their enduring legacy serve as a testament to the human spirit. This book is a humble attempt to honor their memory and to ensure that their contributions to the Allied victory in World War II are never forgotten. It is also dedicated to our families, who endured the anxieties and uncertainties of war, and whose unwavering support sustained these Soldiers during a time of profound challenge. Their strength and love are a powerful tribute to the human spirit, and this book is dedicated to them as well. Finally, this is dedicated to all those who have served and continue to serve in the military, embodying sacrifice, bravery and a commitment to a cause greater than themselves. Their dedication warrants acknowledgement and respect. The valor and sacrifice they exhibit, past and present, continues to inspire future generations.

Preface

The story of Ernest V. Orsi and Company L, 317th Infantry Regiment, during the intense fighting for Mont Saint Jean remains largely untold. This book aims to rectify that omission, offering a detailed and deeply researched account of their experiences. Drawing upon primary sources – stories told by my grandfather, official records, and maps – we strived to reconstruct the battle's progression from the perspective of the men who fought there. It was a privilege to delve into these materials, to hear the voices of these Soldiers, and to gain a glimpse into their lives and experiences. This project was not without its challenges. Many records were incomplete, and others were fragmented, requiring meticulous piecing together to create a cohesive narrative. However, through this process, an incredible story emerged – a narrative of valor, resilience, and camaraderie under extreme pressure.

While this work focuses on my grandfather and that of military operations, I have also sought to explore the human cost of war, focusing on the Soldiers' fears, hopes, and anxieties. This story is not just about tactics and strategy; it is about the men who fought, and the lasting impact of their service. We hope that this book serves not only as a valuable contribution to the historical record, but also as a moving tribute to the bravery and sacrifice of Company L, 317th Infantry Regiment.

Acknowledgements

I am deeply grateful to all of our Service Members and Veterans. Your service and sacrifices are greatly appreciated and will never be forgotten.

Thank you to the 80th Infantry Division Veterans Association. Your website and archived information provided me the resources and tools to put this book together.

A special thanks to my wife Bree and our children Brayden, Landon, and Avery, for your patience and understanding during the long hours I spent researching and writing this special book.

I extend my sincere thanks to my mother Catherine Prezioso, my aunt Veronica Orsi, and my brother Nicholas Prezioso for sharing various stories, information, and photos from Poppy. I couldn't have finished this project without your assistance.

Introduction

The battle of Mont Saint Jean, while perhaps not as famous as other World War II battles, stands as a crucial engagement in the Allied push across Europe. Mont Saint Jean is a scenic hill located in Jeandelincourt, France, that was given the objective name of Hill 407. The hilltop offers a wide-view overlooking Jeandelincourt, Sivry, Moivrons, and the Moselle countryside. This book focuses on the pivotal role played by Company L, 317th Infantry Regiment, during this critical phase of the campaign. Their actions were instrumental in securing Mont Saint Jean, and understanding their experiences provides a valuable insight into the complexities and challenges of urban warfare. Beyond the strategic and tactical analyses, this narrative delves into the human dimension of conflict. It seeks to illuminate the experiences of ordinary Soldiers facing extraordinary circumstances– the fear, the exhaustion, the camaraderie that bound them together. Through careful examination of primary sources, including personal letters, unit diaries, and official reports, we can reconstruct the day-to-day realities of combat and the psychological toll of war. This isn't simply a chronicle of military actions; it is an exploration of the human cost, the emotional landscape experienced by these men, and the enduring impact of their experiences. By integrating detailed tactical analyses with personal narratives, this book aims to provide a comprehensive and nuanced understanding of Company L's contribution to the Allied victory, emphasizing the importance of remembering the sacrifices made by these brave individuals. The chapters that follow will detail their training, their deployment to the European Theater, the build-up to the battle, the harrowing assault itself, and the lasting impact of their experiences on the men and their families. The book also explores the logistical difficulties faced, the medical challenges of the battlefield, and the psychological toll of war. Ultimately, this book aims to provide a nuanced and engaging account of a critical moment in World War II, highlighting the courage, sacrifice and resilience of the men of Company L, 317th Infantry Regiment.

PART I

TRAIN & DEPLOY

Formation & Training
of the Regiment

The 317th Infantry Regiment, a unit destined to play a pivotal role in the European Theater of World War II, emerged from the crucible of American mobilization. Its formation, like that of many other units, was a whirlwind of activity, a testament to the nation's rapid expansion of its armed forces in response to the escalating global conflict. The regiment's genesis can be traced back to August 1917 during World War I, where they were first organized at Camp Lee, Virginia. Later in 1921, the 317th Infantry was reconstituted and assigned to the 80th "Blue Ridge" Infantry Division, and allotted to the Third Corps Area. Then in July of 1942, the regiment was activated for World War II.

In early 1944, Ernest V. Orsi was registered and selected by Draft Board 273 to serve in the Army, and later departed for Camp Dix, NJ.

Farewell Sketch by Ernest V. Orsi on January 21, 1944.

In February 1944, he reported to the Camp Dix Reception Center to be in-processed and staged with other draftees prior to attending Basic Training. After five days of reception center

Camp Dix, Reception Center Headquarters, 1944.

activities he was transported with other recruits to the Infantry Replacement Training Center in Camp Wolters, TX.

Front of a Postcard from Camp Wolters, TX.

The early days of the Regiment at Camp Wolters were characterized by the intense, often grueling, process of basic training. This involved a rigorous 17-week curriculum designed to transform civilians into Soldiers, capable of enduring the physical and mental hardships of combat. The training regime encompassed a range of disciplines: marksmanship, physical conditioning, fieldcraft, and tactical maneuvers. Their training day would begin at 4:45am and ended at 8pm with a relentless focus on instilling discipline, teamwork, and combat proficiency.

Private Ernest V. Orsi, Camp Wolters, TX, 1944.

The importance of marksmanship training cannot be overstated. The 317th's proficiency with their standard-issue rifles, the M1 Garand, would prove crucial in the battles to come. Detailed records of marksmanship scores and training exercises show the unit's performance improved steadily throughout the training period. Beyond the technical aspects of shooting, the training emphasized the psychological element – developing the ability to remain calm and accurate under pressure, a skill that would be tested to its limits on the battlefields of Europe.

Photos of inside and outside the barracks at Camp Wolters, TX, 1944. Photos by Ernest V. Orsi.

Close-order drill, a staple of military training, played a vital role in shaping the regiment's discipline and cohesion. The regimented movements, often repeated endlessly, were not merely a display of military precision; they instilled a sense of order, coordination, and mutual reliance, essential for effective teamwork under fire. The daily routines, meticulously followed, fostered a sense of shared purpose and built the foundations of the unit's collective identity. Many Soldier accounts, while not explicitly focusing on this aspect, often mention the camaraderie fostered by the shared hardships of training.

After Soldiers attended Basic Training, they attended their Advance (Specialized) training for their assigned military occupation. For Ernest Orsi, he attended advance training for Infantrymen at Fort Meade, MD in July of 1944. Similar to a trade school, the advanced training teaches technical skills required for their specific Army job. The training also went beyond the purely physical and technical aspects. Soldiers underwent instruction to operate effectively under duress and in the chaos of combat.

The composition of the 317th Infantry Regiment itself reflected the nature of American military organization during WWII. It consisted of three battalions, each subdivided into companies, including the crucial Company L, whose experiences during the Mont Saint Jean campaign form the central focus of this book. The men who made up Company L represented a microcosm of American society, with backgrounds ranging from rural farm laborers to urban factory workers, reflecting the diverse population from which the unit was drawn.

The cohesive nature of the unit, developed during this period of intense training and preparation, would play a crucial role in the regiment's subsequent performance in the European Theater. The bonds forged in the shared experiences of basic training and pre-deployment exercises created a strong sense of unit identity and mutual trust. This mutual support and trust would be tested, time and again, in the fierce battles that lay ahead. The effectiveness of the 317th in its later campaigns and specifically in the engagement at Mont Saint Jean can, in no small measure, be attributed to the rigorous training and the strong sense of camaraderie fostered during its formative period. The foundations for success at Mont Saint Jean were laid not only on the training grounds but also in the forging of enduring bonds amongst the Soldiers of the 317th. The following chapters will explore how these skills and this spirit of unity translated into action during the regiment's pivotal engagement.

Pvt. Ernest V. Orsi (right) and his mother Ernestina Orsi (left) saying good-bye prior to shipping out. August 1944.

Deployment to the European Theater

In August 1944, the journey across the Atlantic was a stark contrast to the structured routine of training. The troop transport, likely a converted passenger liner or a purpose-built transport ship, offered a cramped and often uncomfortable existence. Hundreds of men, packed into relatively small spaces, endured the constant motion of the sea, the monotonous rhythm of the journey punctuated only by the occasional ship's announcement or the rumble of the engines.

The passage, while uneventful in a military sense, presented a unique set of challenges. Maintaining hygiene in the cramped conditions was difficult, and the constant rocking of the ship contributed to fatigue. The monotony of shipboard life, far removed from the intensity of training, might have even increased tension and anxiety amongst the men. This period, though seemingly less dramatic than the battles to come, played a significant role in shaping the mental and emotional preparedness of the Soldiers. The mental fortitude developed during this prolonged period of waiting would be crucial in the face of the coming horrors of war.

The arrival of Company L in September 1944 on Omaha Beach in Normandy marked a dramatic shift in their experience. The journey's end, with its promise of action and the impending reality of war, brought a mixture of excitement and apprehension. The initial landing, in the disembarkation from the transport ship, would have been a chaotic scene, a stark contrast to the orderly procedures of training.

Omaha Beach. Photo taken by Ernest V. Orsi.

Bunker on the Omaha Beach. Photo taken by Ernest V. Orsi.

The sheer scale of the operation, the volume of men and material being unloaded, would have been overwhelming. Ports were often congested, and the unloading process could take days, adding to the Soldiers' sense of anticipation and uncertainty. Their first impressions of Europe, depending on the port of arrival, varied drastically. Some may have been greeted with the destruction of war already visible, while others may have seen less immediate evidence of the conflict. Anecdotes from Soldier letters would capture the nuances of their initial experiences, ranging from descriptions of the landscape to observations about the local people and the palpable atmosphere of war.

Following disembarkation, the Soldiers of the 317th faced a twenty-day movement from Omaha Beach to Autreville Sur Moselle.

Autreville. Photo taken by Ernest V. Orsi.

This journey introduced the Soldiers to the realities of the European landscape and the stark contrast between the American training grounds and the battle-scarred continent. The Soldiers had to adapt to the start of colder temperatures, different terrain, and perhaps unfamiliar rations. The ability of the regiment to adapt to the harsh European weather and adapt their training skills to the new physical environment would be crucial to their survival and success in combat.

Sniper position in Moselle Sector. Drawing by Ernest V. Orsi.

The detailed account of this period provides the critical backdrop against which the bravery and resilience of Company L will be fully appreciated. The following chapters will delve deeper into the specific engagements that made the 317th, and Company L in particular, a significant force in the European Theater of World War II.

PART II

MONT SAINT JEAN

Battle Intelligence & Strategy

The movement and build-up to the siege of Mont Saint Jean was a period of intense activity, a whirlwind of logistical preparations, strategic planning, and the occupation of various defensive positions that ultimately shaped the 317th Infantry Regiment's role in the battle. The success, or failure, of the operation hinged not only on the bravery and skill of the men on the ground but also on the quality of the intelligence gathered and the effectiveness of the Allied strategic plan. For Company L, nestled within the larger structure of the 317th, this period meant a transition from the anxieties of deployment to the focused intensity of preparing for a crucial engagement.

The strategic planning for the assault on Mont Saint Jean involved a careful consideration of the terrain, enemy defenses, and the available Allied resources. The Allied commanders involved understood the importance of coordinated attacks, air support, and efficient logistical planning. Maps of the region, often supplemented by aerial photographs, were meticulously studied to identify weaknesses in the German defenses and to plan the optimal approach for Allied forces. The objective was not only to capture Mont Saint Jean but also to minimize casualties among Allied troops.

The 317th Infantry Regiment, and specifically Company L, played a crucial role within the overall Allied plan. The regiment was assigned a specific sector of attack, considering its strengths, its level of training, and the anticipated difficulty of the terrain. The detailed operational orders issued to the regiment would have described the objectives, the planned timeline, the allocated resources, and the coordination with other units. These orders would have outlined the 317th's role in conjunction with neighboring regiments, specifying the timing of attacks, the allocation of artillery support, and the anticipated challenges. The importance of meticulous planning and execution can't be overstated. The strategic plan aimed at a coordinated assault to exploit weaknesses and avoid head-on clashes with heavily fortified positions. This involved careful consideration of the timing and sequence of attacks to achieve a decisive breakthrough.

The anticipated difficulties faced by the 317th included the strength of the German defenses, the potential for heavy casualties, and the possibility of unforeseen problems. Mont Saint Jean, given its strategic importance, was likely heavily fortified with machine-gun nests, artillery emplacements, and well-entrenched infantry positions. The terrain itself might have presented additional challenges, depending on the time of year and weather conditions.

Mont Saint Jean. Photo taken by Ernest V. Orsi.

The information available to the 317th's leadership before the assault likely included maps, intelligence summaries, aerial photographs, and the operational orders outlining the regiment's specific role. This information would have been crucial in allowing company commanders to brief their troops, explain the objectives, and prepare their men for the challenges ahead. The briefing sessions likely included discussions of enemy defenses, the planned approach, and procedures for coordinating with neighboring units. The overall atmosphere leading up to the assault would likely have been one of intense anticipation and a quiet determination, a blend of nervous energy and focused resolve.

The build-up to the battle for Mont Saint Jean was not merely a matter of military preparations; it was a delicate balancing act of acquiring, interpreting, and utilizing available information to formulate a coherent and effective strategic plan. The success of the 317th Infantry Regiment, and Company L in particular, depended on both the courage and skills of the Soldiers and the quality of the intelligence and strategic planning that had preceded the assault.

The coming conflict would test every aspect of their training, preparation, and ultimately, their resilience in the face of a relentless enemy.

Preparation for the Assault

The days leading up to the assault on Mont Saint Jean were far from tranquil for Company L. The relative calm of the preceding weeks, punctuated by the distant rumble of artillery and the occasional sniper fire, shattered as the intensity of the impending battle began to manifest. Intelligence reports, often fragmented and

Enemy foxhole on Mont Saint Jean. Photo taken by Ernest V. Orsi.

unreliable, painted a picture of a heavily fortified enemy position, manned by seasoned troops entrenched in well-prepared defensive works. This intelligence, coupled with aerial reconnaissance that revealed the extent of the German fortifications, heightened the sense of apprehension within the company.

Company L's initial encounters with the enemy were not large-scale engagements but rather a series of smaller skirmishes and probing actions designed to gather more precise intelligence and to assess the enemy's strength and disposition. These actions, while less dramatic than the full-scale assault, were nevertheless crucial in shaping the company's understanding of the challenges they would face. These early encounters frequently involved patrols sent out to scout enemy positions, assess their defenses, and identify potential vulnerabilities that could be exploited during the main assault.

These patrols, composed of highly skilled and experienced Soldiers, ventured into the no-man's-land separating the Allied and German lines. Their mission profiles ranged from simple reconnaissance to attempts to disrupt enemy communication lines or gather information about their troop deployments, supply lines, and potential reserves. The accounts from these patrol members, often meticulously documented in their personal diaries and later recounted in post-war interviews, provide a harrowing glimpse into the perilous nature of their task. They describe navigating treacherous terrain under the constant threat of enemy fire, relying on stealth, sharp senses, and precise marksmanship to avoid detection and engage with enemy outposts.

A terrain feature away from Mont Saint Jean.
Drawing by Ernest V. Orsi.

One recurring theme in these accounts is the ingenuity and resourcefulness displayed by the

Soldiers in adapting to the unpredictable challenges they faced. They frequently describe modifying their equipment to better suit the terrain, creating improvised camouflage, and developing innovative tactics to overcome enemy defenses. The creation of improvised explosive devices, for example, using readily available materials, was often mentioned as a crucial method for disrupting enemy patrols or destroying smaller fortifications. The resourceful use of captured enemy equipment and the adaptation of standard-issue weaponry to suit specific tasks underscore the Soldiers' adaptability and improvisational skills.

Casualties, sadly, were an unavoidable consequence of these pre-assault operations. While the exact number of casualties sustained during these initial skirmishes remains difficult to ascertain definitively due to incomplete records, the personal accounts of surviving patrol members paint a grim but realistic picture. These accounts describe fierce close-quarters combat, with significant losses caused by well-placed enemy fire, surprise attacks from concealed positions, and the use of booby traps. The Soldiers often faced the enemy in situations of limited visibility, with engagements frequently occurring at night or in dense vegetation.

These patrol encounters served a vital purpose beyond gathering intelligence. They provided valuable combat experience for the men of Company L, allowing them to test their training and refine their tactical responses under actual combat conditions. The lessons learned during these skirmishes, often brutal and unforgiving, proved invaluable during the main assault on Mont Saint Jean. The practical application of these lessons under pressure shaped the Soldiers' decision-making processes, increasing their tactical awareness and proficiency in executing complex maneuvers. The experience forged a stronger bond among the men, fostering a shared understanding of the challenges ahead and strengthening their collective resolve.

The preparation for the main assault also included intensive training exercises, designed to refine the company's tactical proficiency and to ensure seamless coordination with supporting units. These exercises simulated various scenarios, replicating the likely challenges they would face during the assault. The focus was on honing their skills in close-quarters combat, breaching heavily fortified defensive positions, and coordinating their actions with artillery barrages and armored support. The exercises also emphasized the importance of maintaining communication, minimizing casualties, and efficiently managing resources.

The logistical preparation for the assault was equally crucial. Ensuring that the company had adequate supplies of ammunition, food, water, medical supplies, and replacement personnel was a significant undertaking, requiring meticulous planning and efficient coordination with the larger logistical network. The accounts from Soldiers detail the constant efforts made to maintain supply lines, overcoming challenges posed by the terrain and the ever-present threat of enemy attacks. The successful delivery of necessary supplies was paramount, not only for sustaining the company's combat effectiveness but also for maintaining the Soldiers' morale and fighting spirit.

The psychological preparation for the impending assault was just as important as the tactical and logistical preparations. The company commanders understood the profound impact that the stress and uncertainty of battle could have on the Soldiers. The measures taken included briefing sessions designed to instill confidence, reinforce their training, and to foster a sense of unity and purpose within the unit. The commanders aimed to address the psychological challenges posed by the intense pressures of combat, equipping their Soldiers with the mental resilience needed to overcome their fears and maintain their fighting spirit amidst extreme circumstances.

An afternoon of September 21, 1944.
Drawing by Ernest V. Orsi.

The initial encounters with the enemy, the intensive training exercises, and the meticulous logistical and psychological preparations were all interwoven elements of Company L's readiness for the assault on Mont Saint Jean. These preparatory measures not only enhanced the company's tactical and logistical capabilities but also cultivated a strong sense of cohesion and resilience among its members. The experiences leading up to the main assault shaped the company's character, fortifying their resolve and solidifying their preparedness for the formidable challenges that lay ahead. The intense pressure of the pre-assault period, despite its inherent dangers and losses, served as a crucial

A counter-attack on September 22, 1944. Drawing by Ernest V. Orsi.

crucible in which the men of Company L were forged into a tightly knit, battle-hardened unit, ready to face the horrors and demands of the impending battle. Their readiness, a testament to thorough preparation and unwavering resolve, would be crucial in determining their success in the assault to come.

A counter-attack on September 23, 1944. Drawing by Ernest V. Orsi.

Taking the Hill

On September 27, 1944, the 317th Infantry Regiment were ordered to hold defensive positions on the high ground south of line Morey-Bratte-Vill (Villers-les-Moivrons). The 3rd Battalion (Company L) was on the right, 1st Battalion on the left, and 2nd Battalion in reserve was south of Montenoy.

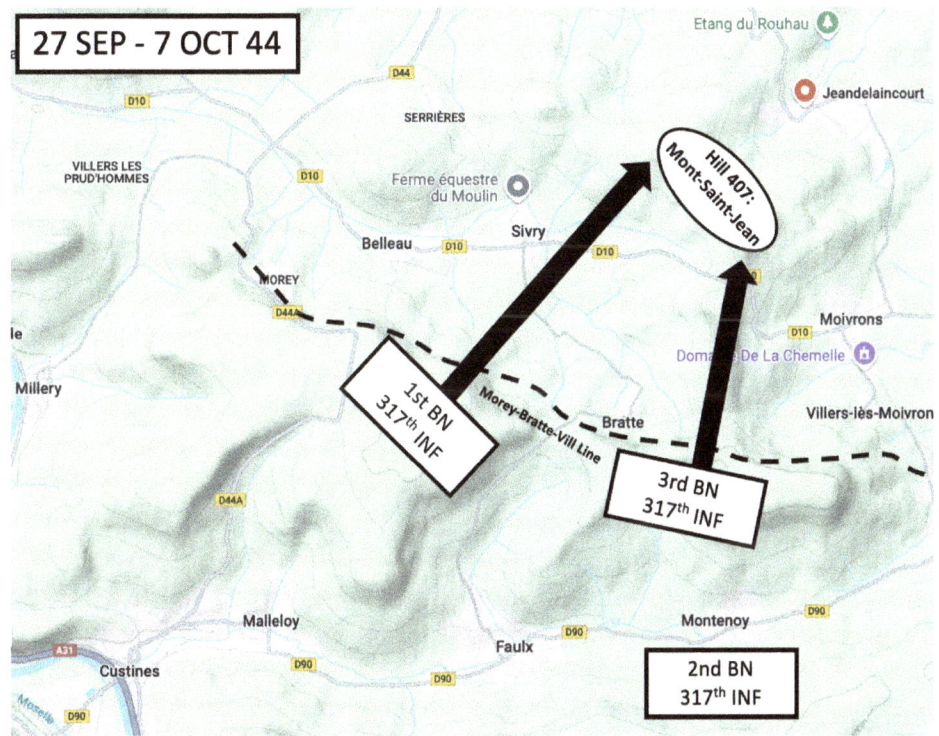

Positions and attack movement of the 317th Infantry Regiment. Diagram by Alexander Prezioso. Background from Google Maps.

The following day the regiment was ordered to conduct patrols and hold defensive positions on the high ground south of Mont Saint Jean. On September 30, the regiment was ordered to stay in place. A new Regiment Commanding Officer changed from Colonel A. Donald Cameron to Colonel Warfield M. Lewis on October 3, 1944.

The air hung heavy with anticipation, a palpable tension that vibrated through the ranks. Two days later the infantry regiments began to readjust their positions and received the division order for the attack on October 8th. The objective: to secure a crucial strategic foothold on the mountain, a formidable German strongpoint that commanded the surrounding terrain. The meticulously planned assault on Mont Saint Jean was about to begin, just as a squadron of P-47s bombed and strafed Mont Saint Jean. Republic P-47 Thunderbolts were armed with eight .50 caliber machine guns and bomb loads of 2,500 pounds. The body style of the aircraft replicated the shape of milk jugs at the time, where it earned its nickname as the 'jug."

In the early morning of October 8, 1944, the first wave of the assault, moved forward under the cover of darkness. 3rd Battalion's task, that included Company L, was to seize the southern portion of Mont-Saint-Jean, with 1st Battalion

Strafing Mont Saint Jean. Drawing by Ernest V. Orsi.

seizing the northern portion, and with 2nd
Battalion supporting the attack as a reserve near
the town of Morly. Other elements of the 317th
moved to Moivron and Jeandelincourt as well for
support. The initial advance was characterized by a
calculated slowness, a deliberate pace designed to
minimize exposure to enemy fire. They moved in
small, tightly knit squads, utilizing the limited
cover provided by the open terrain and scattered
vegetation. The advance was a delicate dance
between speed and stealth, a balancing act between
the urgency of the mission and the necessity of
maintaining tactical discipline.

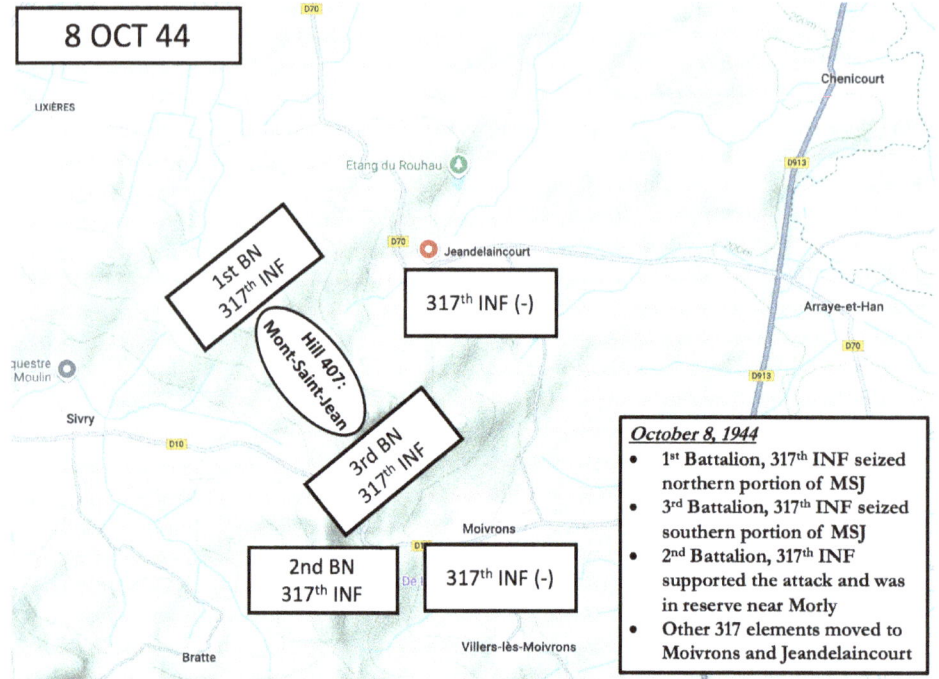

Positions of the 317th after seizing Mont Saint Jean.
Diagram by Alexander Prezioso. Background from Google Maps.

The terrain itself proved to be a significant challenge. The slopes of Mont Saint Jean were steep and uneven, treacherous underfoot, and riddled with obstacles that hampered the progress of the advancing Soldiers. The German defenders, alerted by the approaching sounds of the advancing men, responded with a furious barrage of machine gun and mortar fire.

The initial wave of the assault faced immediate and intense resistance. Machine-gun fire, accurately placed from well-concealed positions, inflicted casualties in the leading ranks. Mortar shells, landing with devastating effect, created chaos in the advancing lines. The men of Company L found themselves immediately engaged in brutal close-quarters combat, the carefully rehearsed battle plans needing immediate improvisation and adaptability. The initial planned tactical maneuver – a swift flanking maneuver to outflank the German right flank – was disrupted by the unexpected intensity of the enemy fire. This forced the assaulting troops to modify their approach and to seek alternate routes up Mont Saint Jean.

Taking Mont Saint Jean. Drawing by Ernest V. Orsi.

The sheer volume of fire from the German defenders was staggering. Our grandfather described a loudness of explosions and the relentless whine of machine guns, a terrifying symphony of death that threatened to overwhelm the advance. The intensity of the fighting was such that many Soldiers described feeling as though they were moving through a hail of bullets and shrapnel. Cover was hard to find and when found, it was often temporary.

The early setbacks, while demoralizing, did not break the spirit of Company L. The men, hardened by weeks of intense training and relentless patrol encounters, clung to their positions, doggedly advancing despite the heavy casualties. Their response was characterized by a remarkable blend of courage and tactical flexibility. Individual Soldiers demonstrated remarkable bravery, charging forward under heavy fire to clear enemy positions. The squad leaders adapted quickly to the changing battlefield situation, directing their men to seek cover, exploiting momentary lulls in the enemy fire, and improvising alternate routes.

The use of hand grenades proved crucial in clearing out enemy bunkers and strongpoints. The Soldiers, utilizing their training, hurled grenades with lethal accuracy, disrupting enemy fire and neutralizing fortified positions. The coordinated use of explosives by the engineers proved instrumental in creating breaches in the German defensive lines, creating critical avenues for the advance. Close-quarters combat was often brutal and hand-to-hand fighting, using bayonets and rifle butts, was commonplace.

Despite these challenges, Company L managed to exploit several weaknesses in the enemy's defenses, utilizing the terrain to their advantage. The early gains were hard-fought and costly, bought with the blood and sacrifice of many brave Soldiers.

Regaining Mont Saint Jean. Drawing by Ernest V. Orsi.

As the first day of the assault ended, the men of Company L found themselves clinging to their hard-won gains on the slopes of Mont Saint Jean. But despite the casualties and the setbacks, their tenacity and determination remained unbroken. They had achieved a foothold, albeit a bloody one, and they were ready to resume the fight at dawn, their resolve strengthened by the shared experiences and the comradeship forged in the crucible of battle. The initial phase of the assault had provided a brutal yet invaluable lesson: the conquest of Mont Saint Jean would be a hard-fought battle of attrition, requiring not only tactical skill but also unwavering courage and relentless determination. The fighting was far from over, but Company L had shown their mettle. They had proven their ability to adapt, to overcome adversity, and to fight with unwavering bravery in the face of overwhelming odds.

The night brought a grim reckoning. The wounded were tended to under the flickering light of lanterns, the air heavy with the stench of blood and smokeless explosive. The dead were solemnly prepared for burial, their sacrifices a stark reminder of the brutal reality of war. The surviving members of Company L huddled together, finding solace in shared experiences and in the unwavering camaraderie that had bound them together throughout the ordeal. The night was punctuated by the distant sounds of artillery and the sporadic bursts of machine-gun fire, a constant reminder of the danger that still lurked.

Searching captured enemies on Mont Saint Jean.
Drawing by Ernest V. Orsi.

The capture of Mont Saint Jean was not a single, decisive action but a series of interconnected battles fought over days, a testament to the perseverance of Company L and the intensity of the German defense. The opening stages of the assault, however, defined the tone of the entire battle. It was a baptism by fire, a brutal introduction to the realities of modern warfare. The initial challenges faced – the treacherous terrain, the intense enemy fire, and the communication difficulties – underscored the immense difficulties involved in securing the

A fighting position in Jeandelaincourt with a view of Mont Saint Jean. Drawing by Ernest V. Orsi.

strategic position. The success that Company L achieved in spite of these challenges, however, speaks volumes of their determination, training, and the profound camaraderie that allowed them to achieve what seemed like the impossible. Over

1,200 prisoners were captured, with many Germans wounded and killed.

Consolidation & Evacuation

On the morning of October 9, 1944, the roar of battle faded into a low, unsettling hum, as the regiment conducted movement northeast to seize the towns of Cheincourt and Letricount. The immediate aftermath was a chaotic blend of relief and exhaustion. Soldiers, faces grimy and etched with fatigue, collapsed where they stood, their weapons discarded, bodies trembling from the adrenaline finally subsiding. The Soldiers, many still emotionally raw from the intense fighting, had to maintain constant vigilance, their nerves frayed by the lingering echoes of battle. This constant state of alert added an extra layer of strain to an already exhausted unit.

Once the regiment seized Cheincourt and Letricount, the tending to the wounded was an immediate and pressing concern. The company's medics, working tirelessly under makeshift operating conditions, struggled to cope with the sheer number of casualties. The medics, working with limited supplies and equipment, performed life-saving procedures under the constant threat of further attack, demonstrating a level of dedication that defied description. Their commitment went beyond the call of duty and speaks volumes about the dedication of the medical personnel who were part of this battle.

Beyond the immediate physical casualties, the psychological toll on the men was immense. The horrors they had witnessed—the intense close-quarters fighting, the sight of fallen comrades, the relentless barrage of enemy fire—left deep scars. Many Soldiers displayed signs of trauma, their emotional equilibrium severely shaken. Sleep became a distant memory, haunted by nightmares and flashbacks of the brutal encounter. The emotional cost of the battle often went unrecognized and left a lasting impact on the Soldiers, who had faced relentless danger and extreme levels of stress.

The capture of Mont Saint Jean was a significant victory, but its consolidation and aftermath presented a distinct set of challenges, demanding resilience, organizational skill, and unwavering dedication. The story of Company L's experience extends beyond the fierce fighting itself; it encompasses the difficult days that followed, the struggle to recover, the immense psychological toll, and the unwavering commitment of Soldiers who persevered through the hardships. The battle for Mont Saint Jean, therefore, is not just a narrative of combat, but a comprehensive account of courage, sacrifice, and the enduring human spirit in the face of overwhelming odds. The story of Company L embodies the true cost of war and pays tribute to the resilience and strength of its Soldiers.

The official casualty reports, compiled in the grim aftermath of the battle for Mont Saint Jean, painted a stark picture of the human cost. For Company L, the victory was dearly bought. The figures, stark and unforgiving, spoke of shattered lives and families left behind: twenty-seven men killed in action, fifty-two wounded, and eight missing in action. These numbers, however, represented more than just statistics; they represented the individual sacrifices made by courageous Soldiers, each with their own stories, hopes, and dreams.

Among one of the 52 wounded, was our grandfather, Private Ernest V. Orsi. His status changed from duty to absent sick (line of duty – non-battle casualty). He was immediately sent to the 80th Division's Clearing Station for immediate care for a severe case of trench foot. He was then later sent to the 119th General Hospital in Blandford, England to recover for his injuries.

In World War II, with the constant movement, and fighting, Soldiers were unable to wash clothes and keep clean as often as they should have. Between the changes in temperature and weather, body sweat, and movement through wet terrain, it was difficult for Soldiers to keep their feet dry and clean for extended periods of time. Many Soldiers developed the condition of trench foot, which caused them numbness, pain, redness, and severe swelling.

Some Soldiers, like Private Orsi, developed such severe cases where they could no longer stand or walk, and had to be evacuated. You could only imagine the experience and pain our Soldiers had to endure while fighting.

The battle for Mont Saint Jean serves as a lasting tribute to the courage and sacrifice of the men who fought there, a reminder of the human cost of war and the enduring legacy of their contributions.

Reflections

The preceding chapters have detailed the arduous journey of my grandfather and Company L, 317th Infantry Regiment, during the intense fighting for Mont Saint Jean. We've had several private and detailed conversations with our grandfather about his experience during World War II. We also researched and traced the movements of the 317th Regiment. analyzed their tactics, and explored their experiences that shaped their collective narrative. Yet, beyond the tactical maneuvers and strategic objectives lies a deeper story—the human cost of war, the enduring legacy of those who served, and the profound impact of their sacrifice. This concluding reflection seeks to encapsulate those less tangible yet equally crucial aspects of their story.

The capture of Mont Saint Jean, while a significant tactical victory, came at a considerable price. The psychological toll of war extends far beyond the immediate battlefield. The horrors witnessed, the comrades lost, and the constant threat to life leave an indelible mark on the psyche. The veterans of Company L, like our grandfather and the countless veterans who fought in World War II, carried the invisible wounds of war long after they returned home. Many struggled with post-traumatic stress, a condition often misunderstood and untreated in those years. The challenges they faced upon returning to civilian life, attempting to readjust to a world vastly different from the one they left behind, add another layer to their experience, further highlighting the immense human cost of their service. The transition back to civilian life often involved a silent struggle, a battle fought on a different front, one marked by internal turmoil and a disconnection from a society that, however grateful, rarely understood the true weight of their experiences.

Beyond the individual experiences, the battle of Mont Saint Jean offers critical lessons in military strategy and tactical decision-making. The successes and failures encountered by Company L, along with those of their allied units and the opposing forces, provide valuable case studies for military analysts and historians alike. The effectiveness of specific tactics, the importance of communication and coordination, and the challenges posed by the terrain and enemy defenses all serve as valuable teaching points.

Analysis of the battle, however, should extend beyond pure military strategy. It should delve into the impact of leadership, the importance of morale and unit cohesion, and the vital role of logistics in supporting sustained combat operations. The resilience of Company L in the face of adversity stands as a testament to the strength of human spirit and the power of effective leadership, even under extreme pressure.

The enduring legacy of Company L, 317th Infantry Regiment, and their involvement in the capture of Mont Saint Jean transcends the immediate historical context. Their story serves as a powerful reminder of the human cost of war, the importance of remembering those who served, and the valuable lessons learned from their experiences. Their narrative compels a deeper understanding of the challenges faced by Soldiers, the psychological toll of combat, and the lasting impact of war on individuals, families, and communities. Their experiences continue to resonate, reminding us of the enduring strength of the human spirit and the need for peace. The meticulous account of their journey emphasizes the importance of preserving historical memory, ensuring their sacrifice is not only remembered, but understood and deeply appreciated. This is a reminder not just of their heroism but of the human element intrinsic to any conflict, underscoring the critical need for humanity in war's wake. By studying their experiences, we deepen our understanding of the human condition and learn to better safeguard the future. The story of Company L is, ultimately, a story of courage, sacrifice, and the unwavering spirit of those who served, a legacy that deserves to be remembered and cherished.

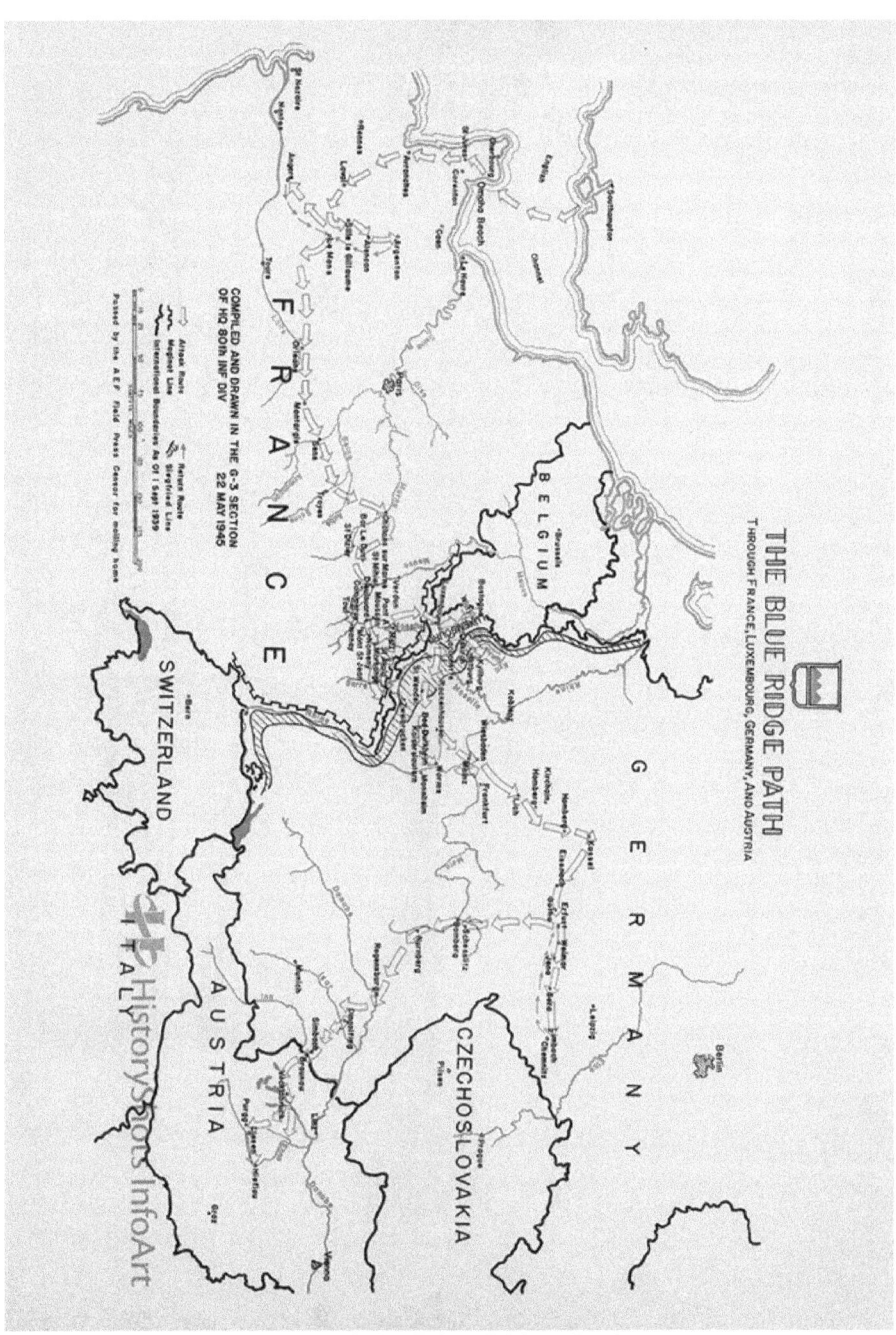

Map of the Blue Ridge Path.

PART III

RETURNING HOME

Follow-on Assignments

Following Private Orsi's medical treatment in England, he was transferred to B Battery, 775th Field Artillery Battalion. The battery was a part of General Patton's Third Army, and were stationed in northern France and eastern Germany from 1942-1945. The battery's mission was to provide artillery support. Private Orsi joined the unit in Flaxweiler, Luxembourg in January 1945, and then the unit moved forward to Bunglegenfeld,  Germany in May of 1945 when the Germans officially surrendered to Allied Forces.

Weapons Platoon(-), L Company, 317th Infantry Regiment with Light Machine Guns and 60mm Mortars in Windscharsten, Austria. May 10, 1945. Photo by Ernest V. Orsi.

In September of 1945, Private Orsi was transferred to the 407th Antiaircraft Artillery (AAA) Gun Battalion located in Paris, France. The battalion was known as the "Buzz Bomb Kings," and was commanded by Lieutenant Colonel Cleo E. Coles. Upon Private Orsi's transfer to the unit, the 407th was in a non-operational status, and opened a rest camp in Paris for Soldiers to wait until they began departing back to the United States. Private Orsi remained in Paris for the next five months until he departed to Fort Dix, NJ for demobilization in March of 1946.

Anti-aircraft artillery team. Photo by Ernest V. Orsi.

In a foxhole. Photo by Ernest V. Orsi.

Artillery - King of Battle! Photo by Ernest V. Orsi.

Crew with the M2 Browning Machine Gun. Photos by Ernest V. Orsi.

Demobilization

Following the surrender of Germany to the Allies on May 8, 1945, the United States Army was faced with the challenge of bringing home millions of service members overseas. Part of the challenge was organizing the movement of personnel back home in a fair and efficient manner over a twelve-month period. In order to do this, the Army developed the Adjusted Service Rating Score.

The Adjusted Service Rating Score was a point-based assessment that rated each Soldier individually on a set of criteria. Soldiers with the highest number of points were the priority with returning home first. The scores were calculated on an Adjusted Service Rating Card based on the following:

- 1 Point - For each month in service in the Army
- 1 Point - For each month in service overseas
- 5 Points - Per each campaign
- 5 Points - For each medal for merit or valor (Silver Star for example), or Purple Heart

- 12 Points - For each dependent child 18 years or younger. Maximum allowed points were 36 for up to 3 dependent children.

Once scores were calculated, the Army developed an order of merit list from the highest scores to the lowest. Although this system was straight forward, it still presented different types of administrative and morale issues. The system was an administrative nightmare to ensure there was no misinterpretations, misinformation communicated to the field, and rapidly collecting the cards back to generate the list.

Additionally, the multiplier for dependents was reported by many Soldiers as unfair and too high. For example, a Soldier who could have been overseas for two years, would have a significant number of lower points than a new Soldier arriving in theatre with three dependents. The newer Soldier could have 36 points advantage over the Soldier.

CHART II

ADJUSTED SERVICE RATING CARD

Name .... Army Serial No............................

Unit .... Arm or Service.......................

Primary Mil. Occupational Specialty: Title .... SSN.............

Type of credit:

	No.	Multiply by	Credits
1. SERVICE CREDIT No. of months in Army since Sept. 16, 1940.........................			
2. OVERSEA CREDIT No. of months served overseas..			
3. COMBAT CREDIT No. of decorations and Bronze Service Stars........................			
4. PARENTHOOD CREDIT No. of children under 18 years old.....................................			

TOTAL CREDITS ....

READ INSTRUCTIONS on reverse
side before filling card out.   CERTIFIED BY ....

Form Emerg. No. 246–8717

Adjusted Service Rating Card, Form Emergency. No. 246-8717

After patiently waiting in Paris for 5 months, Private First Class Orsi, returned back to the United States in March of 1946 to demobilize through Camp Dix, NJ.

The Demobilization of United States Armed Forces after the Second World War began with the defeat of Germany in May 1945 and continued through 1946. The United States had more than 12 million men and women in the armed forces at the end of World War II, of whom 7.6 million were stationed abroad. The American public demanded a rapid demobilization and Soldiers protested the slowness of the process. Many Service Members were stuck overseas until reinforcements could arrive in theatre, as well as the rotation of millions of personnel getting shipped back.

Private First Class Ernest V. Orsi.

BIOGRAPHY

Dr. Ernest V. Orsi

Dr. Ernest Vincenzo Orsi was born on August 10, 1922 in New York City to Augustus and Ernestina Orsi. At the time of his birth, his parents owned a gas station. A year later, Ernest left America with his father to live with his extended family in Italy due to his mother's illness.

Ernest V. Orsi working at his father's gas station.

Dr. Orsi returned five years later to the United States to rejoin his mother and father and attend elementary school. While growing up, he loved reading books by Mark Twain, especially "Tom Sawyer." At a young age he had aspirations to become a doctor, and his motto was, "Be prepared!"

In 1944, Dr. Orsi was drafted at age twenty-two to serve in the Army as a Rifleman in the European Theater, Third Army, 80th Division during World War II. During his deployment overseas, he served in a variety of units including: Company L, 317th Infantry Regiment, B Battery, 775th Field Artillery Battalion, and the 407th Antiaircraft Artillery (AAA) Gun Battalion.

Several years after returning home from the war, Dr. Orsi was set up on a blind date with Clara Hitscherich by a mutual friend who worked at Saint Vincent's School of Nursing. The two immediately fell in love, and married after three months of dating.

Dr. Orsi graduated from Queens College and then earned his master's degree from Fordham University. After having their first child, Edward, the two then moved to Saint Louis, Missouri where Dr. Orsi earned his doctorate in Microbiology at Saint Louis University. While living in Saint Louis and attending school, Clara gave birth to daughters Veronica and Catherine.

Upon graduating from Saint Louis University, they moved to Pearl River, NY where Dr. Orsi assisted in the development of an oral polio vaccine at Lederle Laboratories and had their final and fourth child, Joseph.

Later on, Dr. Orsi joined the Virus Diagnostic Unit of the New York City Health Department. He spent the major part of his career as professor, research scientist, and a highly regarded mentor to graduate students in the Biology Department at Seton Hall University in South Orange, N.J.

When Dr. Orsi retired, he volunteered at St. Agnes School in Lake Placid, N.Y., as a kindergarten and first grade teacher's aide. He performed science demonstrations for a future generation of microbiologists.

On Sunday, July 31, 2011, at his home, Dr. Orsi passed away at the age of 88, and was later buried at Ascension Cemetery in Airmont, NY. He was recently, joined by his wife, Clara, who died on February 15, 2025.

Dr. Ernest & Clare Orsi married on April 30, 1949.

References

E. Orsi, personal communication (no date).

80th Division Veterans Association:
https://www.80thdivision.com

"The Points Were All That Mattered: The US Army's Demobilization After World War II," The National World War II Museum – New Orleans:
https://www.nationalww2museum.org/war/articles/points-system-us-armys-demobilization

www.ingramcontent.com/pod-product-compliance
Lightning Source LLC
Chambersburg PA
CBHW040148010726
47475CB00039B/495